It is empty country on Topo and Castaneda who chronicled Coronado's expedition writes of getting completely lost because the land was so level. The High Plains were formed by the outwash of sediments coming down from the Rockys in the tertiary period and are, geologically the youngest formation in Texas except for the coast. The vegetation on this alluvial table is primarily short and mid grasses Blue grama and Buffalo grass. It is the land of the Bison and Antelope and today is home to the last free-ranging pure blooded buffalo in America, saved from extinction by Charles Goodnight himself.

TEXAS LOST

To Jim and Dawn Scott —

Thank you both for your great interest in the Outdoors. Lets make sure it is still there for our kids.

Andrew Sansom
February, 1996

TEXAS
LOST

Vanishing Heritage

By Andrew Sansom

Photographs by Wyman Meinzer

Edited by Jan Reid

Foreword by Bob Armstrong

Parks and Wildlife Foundation of Texas, Inc.
P.O. Box 15097
Dallas, Texas 75201-0097

Library of Congress Cataloging-in-Publication Data

Sansom, Andrew.
  Texas lost : vanishing heritage / by Andrew Sansom; edited by
Jan Reid; photographs by Wyman Meinzer.
    p.   cm.
  Includes bibliographical references (p.).
  ISBN 0-9647023-0-4
  1. Natural areas—Texas.   2. Nature conservation—Texas.
  3. Natural areas—Texas—Pictorial works.   I. Reid, Jan.
  II. Meinzer, Wyman.   III. Title.
  QH76.5.T4S26   1995
  333.78′2′09764—dc20   95-33541
                                                        CIP

ISBN 0-9647023-0-4

Editorial and publication management by
The Publishing Partnership, a division of Texas Monthly, Inc.

Design by Barbara Whitehead

This book is dedicated to the employees of the
Texas Parks and Wildlife Department

CONTENTS

ACKNOWLEDGMENTS

This book would not have been possible without the support of a unique institution that has in a few short years become a major factor in Texas conservation issues. Chartered in May 1991, the Parks and Wildlife Foundation of Texas is a nonprofit corporation that partners with the Texas Parks and Wildlife Department to preserve our state's extraordinary natural and cultural heritage, as well as expand upon our enormous potential for diverse outdoor recreation.

The mission of the Foundation is to provide private support for critical efforts of the Department and to take a leadership role in preserving Texas' natural resources for the benefit of future generations.

Today—because of the resources provided by the Foundation's partnership initiative with private sector institutions, corporations, and philanthropists, coupled with the Department's businesslike approach to operations—taxpayer support is no longer a necessity. There are no general tax dollars in the Parks and Wildlife Department operations. This strategy mandates that partnerships of all kinds be forged to support the Parks and Wildlife Department's conservation initiatives.

In the spirit of this unique partnership and entrepreneurial strategy, the Foundation leadership provided a loan from its Anheuser Busch Conservation Endowment Fund to allow Wyman Meinzer and me to work together on this project.

Two successive Foundation chairmen, Ed Cox, Jr., and Tim Hixon, have provided steadfast support, along with President Bill Graham and Executive Director Paula Peters. Here in our office, Anne Jones Helbing and Michelle Klaus worked very hard to make sure that Wyman and I stayed on schedule and

Acknowledgments

that the relationships between the Department, the Foundation, and The Publishing Partnership stayed on an even keel.

The people at The Publishing Partnership were awesome. Cathy Casey, as overall project director, together with Marilyn Plummer and Kristen Bringewald, cracked the whip and saved me by providing the services of our intern Annie Dahl, without whom the research for this book could not have been done. Jan Reid, the editor, was wonderful, helping me to turn my ideas into understanding and reassuring me that I was on the right track, and Jan McInroy, the copyeditor, made sure you could read the material. Barbara Whitehead put the words and pictures together in a way that makes each page seem greater than its component parts, and B. J. Lowe at Gulf Publishing Company made sure that the book reached you in the stores.

Wyman was helped immeasurably by Texas Parks and Wildlife wardens throughout the state, including their boss, Charlie Hensley; Chief Pilot Oscar Lopez; and his colleague Lee Finch. On the ground and in the water, Wardens John Muery, Alton Anderson, Norman Anthony, and Rick Medford transported Wyman all over the state.

Fortunately, some of the most distinguished natural scientists in America work in the Texas Parks and Wildlife Department, and their insights, counsel, and guidance were invaluable. From David Diamond, Jim Neal, and Dr. Larry McKinney, you can learn just about everything you need to know about the biological diversity of Texas. Karen Leslie and Lester Galbreath from the Department's Public Lands Division helped out at Caddo Lake and Fort Griffin.

Colonel Butch Gatlin and his staff at the Galveston District of the U.S. Army Corps of Engineers took me all over the Wallisville project and helped me understand the issues from their perspective.

Up on the Trinity River in Dallas, Neely Kerr helped Wyman get into the forest and discover its secrets. Jim Eidson of The Nature Conservancy of Texas and Parks and Wildlife Commissioner Mickey Burleson led Wyman to the subtle wonders of the Blackland Prairie, and my colleague and dear friend Jim Carrico was Wyman's guide in the Trans-Pecos, where they both saw the magnificent country at close range from the cockpit of Knute Mjolhus's helicopter.

My contribution to this project, modest as it is, could not have been accomplished had not Parks and Wildlife Commissioner Terry Hershey and her husband, Jake, provided me with a historic German retreat at Stonewall where I could hide out and write. These commissioners are my supervisors, and I will always be grateful for their support in this labor of love.

And, speaking of love, my incredible wife, Nona, and Sarah Meinzer put up with a lot on this project, and all we can hope is that they let Wyman and me work together again—because for me, the privilege of working with so accomplished an artist as Wyman Meinzer is akin to playing catch with Nolan Ryan. I'll always be grateful that he allowed me to fill some space on the pages between his remarkable portraits of the most beautiful place in the world.

God Bless Texas.

FOREWORD

Someone once described a Texan as a person with an
oversized sense of place. When I tell people I'm from Texas,
they frequently say, "Oh, yes, I remember Texas. It was hot
there." Well, yes and no. I've been in the Big Bend when it was
a hotter-than-hell-lookin'-for-shade type of place, only to
remember that when I first saw it, a norther had transformed
the landscape into a winter scene of snow-covered cactus.

It's all these places, Texas is. I've known a great part of it.
Not as much as Andy Sansom has, though. He's got the best
job in the world if you like Texas. Read this book, and you'll
know more about what makes a Texan. You'll find diversity
here. This diversity makes our state better. Some of Texas
needs to be left as it is. Whether by motivating an owner or
by providing a way to leave the land alone, we have
to have a way to keep it Texas.

We will, and we'll all be better for it.

Bob Armstrong

Assistant Secretary of the U.S. Department of Interior
Former Texas Land Commissioner
Former Texas Parks and Wildlife Commissioner

October 1995

TEXAS LOST

PROLOGUE

One aspect of our identity as Texans is unsurpassed on any other terrain or by any other people on earth: our sense of place. The strength and diversity of Texas are rooted in an inheritance of lands and waters that constitutes an incredibly rich natural heritage and provides the basis of our identity and culture.

Traditionally, ecologists have recognized ten vegetational areas in Texas, though complex subtleties enrich the landscape within these broad categories. Because of Texas' size, geographic position, natural features, and the widely varied climates it encompasses, the state offers an astounding array of biological diversity. Among its bountiful natural assets are approximately 1,200 vertebrate animals, including 550 species of birds; 5,000 species of vascular plants, including 2,000 wildflowers; and forests, mountains, marshes, prairies, and some of the longest barrier islands in the world.

The landscape of Texas has changed. Very little is pristine now. At one time it was mostly grassland, the southern reaches of the Great Plains, but through the past two centuries or so it has almost all been altered in some way. Thanks to generally enlightened management for the past couple of generations, Texans enjoy an unparalleled variety of outdoor uses and a level of access to them that is equally unexcelled.

Texas ranks first among the states in hunting opportunities and second in fishing. It is today the number one destination in the world for birdwatchers. The impact of these activities on the economy of the state is substantial: In 1993 alone, visitors to Texas state parks spent nearly $200 million, while hunters, anglers, and other wildlife enthusiasts spent almost $4 billion.

Texas' natural advantages form the resource base for a $20 billion tourism and outdoor recreation industry that is now the third-largest industry in the state and a cornerstone of the new economy.

And yet as rich and varied and wonderful as Texas is, seemingly inexorable changes are threatening our natural treasure even as the demands to use it and enjoy it climb ever higher.

Besides its diversity, the most significant characteristic of the land in Texas is that it is privately owned. Unlike other states, Texas entered the Union as an independent nation and thus was in a position to negotiate the retention of its public lands. The early leaders of our state did so, then promptly sold those lands off to retire indebtedness, to finance the fledgling government, to build the Capitol, and to endow the public schools. As a result, some 97 percent of the land area of Texas today is in private ownership, and this fact, more than anything else, accounts for its healthy condition.

On the other hand, in times past the outdoors was more accessible to us because we lived there. Before World War II, 80 percent of all Texans lived on farms and ranches or in rural communities; today 80 percent of us live in cities. Thus, even though good stewardship by private owners has left a legacy of natural wealth, that treasure is less accessible to the majority of Texans than ever before.

At the same time, dogged economic forces threaten stewards of both public and private lands in their efforts to protect the legacy for future generations of Texans and to meet the demands of the present one.

The single most destructive force in the biological environment of Texas today is the continued breakup of family lands brought about by changing economies, inheritance taxes, and a state financial structure that is extremely dependent on property taxes. Throughout much of Central Texas, where only tiny remnants of the native landscape survive today, the average tract size has dropped in this generation alone from thousands of acres to fewer than one hundred in many counties. These areas, which once provided large blocks of land for habitat and outdoor recreation, now consist of tiny plots of introduced vegetation that cannot sustain the native wildlife. Meanwhile, the fear of litigation and regulation has closed off lands whose owners once welcomed outdoor enthusiasts.

At the same time, the 3 percent of Texas that is set aside for the public is also under stress. Declining budgets have reduced the ability of public outdoor recreation agencies at the local, state, and federal levels to operate conservation lands efficiently, or even to maintain the vital infrastructure necessary for public use. Because of the reduced opportunity imposed by the sheer paucity of public land in Texas, what we have is taking a beating even as a new generation of city dwellers increasingly desperate to enjoy the outdoors places more and more demands on it.

Thus, as I write, Texas is in real ways becoming smaller, and extraordinary places that were once accessible and common now reveal themselves as but remnants of a Texas that is passing. These special places are much more to humanity than mere repositories of biological capital—more even than generators of additional economic activity. They are settings in which our children can form values. Their place and meaning for us are magnified as Texans are progressively cut off from the countryside. The loss to us is immeasurable—in more than economic or biological terms. We feel it in our common soul and our aspirations for the next generation.

Chapter One

AUSTIN'S WOODS

played in the ruins as a child, beneath immense live oaks and pecans. The occasional walls, brick cisterns, and piles of rubble were all that remained of the first permanent Anglo settlements in Texas and the land development scheme that set the course for an ensuing political and economic evolution that changed the landscape forever.

Anglo settlement of Texas began in these woods, also known as the Columbia Bottomlands, almost by accident. Stephen F. Austin was basically an impresario, or what today we would call a developer. In 1822, Austin's first boatload of customers left New Orleans to seek their fortunes in Texas. They were scheduled to meet him at the mouth of the Colorado. Instead, their boat, the *Lively*, ran aground on the silt shores of the Brazos at a place now known as Quintana.

Austin thus began the establishment of his colony in a unique, though fairly inhospitable, natural area of Texas. His own plantation, Peach Point, lies near the present town of Jones Creek, on the edge of the only large forest habitat in the state that is directly adjacent to the Gulf of Mexico: the big trees

meet the marshes and savannahs of the Gulf Prairie in a classic ecotone of two distinctly different natural landscapes.

Austin's colonists called these woods "canebrake forests" because of the dense stands of native bamboo that dominated the understory. This ancient jungle was confined to an area that now lies in Brazoria, Matagorda, Fort Bend, and Wharton counties, between the lower Brazos and Colorado river bottoms. The best of these remarkable woodlands flood every year, and one can see the waterline on the trees. The soil is poorly drained black "gumbo," which creates ideal conditions for a rich diversity of hardwood trees, trailing vines, and understory plants of every description, including rare native palms and the ubiquitous palmetto.

But everything is dwarfed by the trees—the dominant stands are live oak, elm, pecan, and green ash. Collectively, they are among the most majestic specimens anywhere in Texas today. Their proximity to the Gulf places them squarely in the flyway of returning spring migrating birds, which, after their exhausting nonstop flight across the Gulf from Central and South America, must make landfall in the forest. In fact, partly because of the existence of Austin's Woods, the Freeport Christmas Bird Count in southern Brazoria County routinely reports the greatest number of species in America, and there are ten active Southern Bald Eagle nests within the area.

In the years since Austin set up his land office at Peach Point, these ancient bottoms have provided the setting for the development of a culture that is as rich as the natural history and as quietly noble as the great trees themselves. When the Emancipation Proclamation ended the short-lived plantation economy on which Austin's colony had depended—this happened in Texas after a two-year delay—the ancient forests became home to five generations of descendants of freedmen, some of whom still own land in the bottoms today at places like Cedar Lane and Four Forks. These landowning African Americans were of sufficient numbers in the late nineteenth century that many of the elected officials from Brazoria County were black, a bit of history not widely recognized until recently.

Today, only tiny remnants of canebrake survive, along Oyster Creek and Caney Creek. Though much of the big timber is gone, numerous fragments of mature forest still accent the region, a few of them extensive. Much is being done to save the quickly diminishing woods. Through a unique philanthropic partnership, Dow Chemical, Phillips Petroleum, Conoco, DuPont, and Seaway Pipeline worked through The Nature Conservancy to establish a Wildlife Management Area at Peach Point, now under the stewardship of Texas Parks and Wildlife. The Conservancy has also moved with Phillips Petroleum and the U.S. Fish and Wildlife Service to save a precious stand of native palms in the bottomlands, and Parks and Wildlife has preserved some of the best forest up the river from Peach Point at Brazos Bend State Park—named by *National Geographic* as one of the ten finest state parks in America. Meanwhile, many private landowners have steadfastly refused to destroy the woodlands in their stewardship.

Despite these efforts, the plight of the great woodlands of the Columbia Bottoms has become urgent. Through the years, the deep, shadowy forests along the Brazos have shaped and enhanced the lives of countless Texans. Since Austin's time, they have shaded the first Capitol of the Republic of Texas at West Columbia and inspired legends of headless ghosts at Bailey's Prairie. But today, the western suburbs of Houston move inexorably south along the river, and time is running out for the big trees under whose branches the Texas Revolution began.

Chapter Two

BOTTOMLAND HARDWOODS

Another route into the new land of Texas for those early Anglo settlers followed the Red River upstream from Louisiana. Stephen F. Austin recommended that his own relatives avoid this route because of its difficulties. The great landscape architect Frederick Law Olmsted, who made the journey in 1853, wrote that the eastern avenue of approach was so wet and inhospitable that commerce was entirely diverted from the region.

Although the topography of the eastern third of Texas is shaped by gently rolling hills, all of the Piney Woods are permeated by low-lying areas that are periodically or even constantly inundated. These flooded bottomlands contain some of the oldest, most beautiful, and most diverse stands of timber in the South, which have been called the Texas rain forests. As many as twenty-four distinct plant communities occur in the bottoms of East Texas, and they, more than any other aspect of the landscape, have given rise to our perception of it and to the unique character of its people and culture.

Nowhere is this relationship between humanity and nature

more striking than at Caddo Lake, an ancient wetland of internationally recognized significance. It was amid the mystical serenity of Caddo Lake that settlers first encountered the word "Tejas." In fact, the Caddo Indians used the word so often to refer to the people whom they believed to be their new friends that the Europeans assumed the Indians were speaking of the land itself, and thus it was named for friendship.

In those days, a vast logjam in the Red River backed Caddo Lake all the way up Cypress Bayou to the trail used by Sam Houston, Davy Crockett, and hundreds of other adventurers and settlers to enter the state. Because the logjam enabled steamboats to make their way through the sodden wilderness as far as Jefferson, that settlement grew into a city and became the pride of a great empire of antebellum commerce, graceful living, culture, and charm. But at the height of the boom, the U.S. Army Corps of Engineers removed the logjam from the river below Shreveport—which was like pulling the plug of a bathtub. Now the bayou was too shallow, and the steamboats would never again come up the Cypress to Jefferson.

Ironically, the destruction of the "Great Raft," as it was called, was only the first of a series of water control actions in the rivers and swamps of East Texas that have destroyed much of the forested bottomlands that existed in the early nineteenth century. And now a new threat is looming. Increasingly, the diverse hardwood timber of the East Texas bottoms is being harvested for the production of paper in the United States and Japan. Portable mills have opened even the smallest tracts of older trees for conversion to chips and pulp.

Preserving the woodlands that remain is critical to the natural heritage of our state. Acre for acre, they are the most diverse and beneficial—and among the most endangered—of the ecosystems in North America. Not only do older trees in these woods provide critical habitat for all species that require hollowed-out trunk cavities for nesting, but they are also essential stops along the great journey of millions of songbirds and other migrants moving to and from Latin America.

These natural resources have enormous economic benefits as well. As floodwaters move through the bottoms, they are

slowed significantly, thus reducing the downstream impact of flood crests, silting, and erosion. The forest is also a very efficient filter for biological pollutants and heavy metals that find their way into the water. And it is the last stand of an incredible cornucopia of wildlife in East Texas, which has provided unparalleled enjoyment and satisfaction to generations of hunters and anglers.

In the face of this ecological crisis, a diverse group of partners has joined forces to save the best of what remains. Champion International has voluntarily committed 50,000 acres of bottomlands in the company inventory to permanent protection. The Little Sandy Hunting and Fishing Club, one of the oldest such organizations in Texas, has led efforts to preserve important woodlands along the Middle Sabine by voluntarily committing its land to permanent protection. Across the river, the Parks and Wildlife Foundation of Texas has teamed up with the Texas Department of Transportation to create a 5,000-acre Wildlife Management Area that, along with Little Sandy, preserves most of the bottomlands identified by the U.S. Fish and Wildlife Service as the most important remaining in Texas.

The same group of partners is at work farther down the Sabine, at Blue Elbow, long prized by conservationists as, along with Caddo Lake, the last of the great cypress tupelo swamps. Situated at the intersection of Interstate 10 and the Sabine River, Blue Elbow lies just out of reach for millions of visitors, but it should soon provide some of them with at least a glimpse of what it was like to arrive in Texas 150 years ago.

Thanks to an extraordinary effort by The Nature Conservancy of Texas, entertainer Don Henley, Congressman Jim Chapman, and strong local support, the Texas Parks and Wildlife Department has acquired 7,000 acres of cypress forest on Caddo Lake, and Jefferson, the area's antebellum jewel, is reemerging as another kind of gateway—a window onto a lost culture and one of the most beautiful places on the earth.

Chapter Three

LOWER
COLORADO

avid Wintermann was my guide. He led me to the blind through the darkness in his rice field in Wharton County, near the Lower Colorado River. As we trudged together across the stubbled terraces to the edge of a small pond, the stars seemed to be reflecting under our feet from the phosphorescent droppings of geese in the black river bottom mud. Later, in the first light of day, we could hear them come awake all around us and take to the skies by the hundreds of thousands. Though our pursuit was intended for ducks rather than geese, the enormous flocks of the larger birds continuously darkened every horizon and all around us dominated the newborn day.

That transcendent experience was enhanced by the company of Wintermann, a man who has measured his life in the rhythm of that immense and timeless migration and dedicated himself to assuring beyond his own existence that it continues. That assurance is totally dependent on continuation of the water supply from the Colorado River.

Lyndon Johnson was another unforgettable son of the

Colorado, who rose to power in a day when its upper reaches in the Hill Country of Texas were among the poorest places in the United States. His political ascendance was based, in part, on the construction of the great dams above Austin, which transformed the river's passage through the flood-prone Deep Balcones Canyons into today's magnificent string of Highland Lakes and brought the region into prosperity. The engine of this transformation has been the Lower Colorado River Authority (LCRA). For most of its sixty-year history, this institution has devoted its extensive resources to dispensing electric power and water to rural and urban residents alike of LBJ's beloved Hill Country. Below the Highland Lakes and Austin, the river was overlooked and neglected.

In between the Hill Country and the rice fields below, the Lower Colorado River flows through three of Texas' biogeographic regions: the Blackland Prairie that lies close against the Balcones Escarpment, the Post Oak Savannah, and the Coastal Prairies and Marshes. Though the Spanish first encountered these reaches more than three hundred years ago, the fertile Lower Colorado river bottoms were settled in later times by Stephen F. Austin's colonists and a culturally rich succession of ethnic Europeans who arrived through Galveston in the late nineteenth century. Here, along the Colorado's banks today, communities from Bastrop to La Grange, Columbus, Wharton, and on downstream reflect a mellow blend of German, Czech, and Spanish culture as diverse as is the changing landscape on the way to the Gulf.

Through most of this passage toward the coast, the river is green and languid. The Hill Country's limestone cliffs yield first to the high chalk bluffs above La Grange, then increasingly to the sandbars and unstable clay banks constructed by the water's relentless movement of sediment and silt. Here in recent years the river has suffered, as the demand for water from the lakes has increased the uncertainty of its flow below the dams. At the same time, dramatic urban growth in and around Austin threatened for a time to exceed the city's capacity to treat the resulting swell of effluent coming into the Colorado. It is ironic that a city so absorbed with its own environmental quality has been

somewhat heedless of the people downriver who are left to deal with its discharged waste.

Today, following an outcry by citizens along the river and increased interest by state government and the LCRA, the Lower Colorado is coming back. Its water quality is improving. And with assistance from the Texas Parks and Wildlife Department, the Lower Colorado River Authority has aggressively begun to develop this stretch of the river for recreation—both by creating opportunities for boaters and anglers to get in and out of it along the way and by guaranteeing a continuous flow of water downstream to the rice fields, the estuaries, and the broadening river itself. Its sandbars once again have become way stations for downriver paddlers, who had not used the river for years. Its pools and eddies provide challenging fishing for smallmouth bass and other species, and its riparian woodlands host a wide diversity of bird life.

To downstream conservationists like David Wintermann, the promise of lasting clean water in the Lower Colorado is more than a physical necessity. It is an article of faith held by Texans, for whom restraint is a lasting value. Many years ago, Wintermann refrained from hunting his lands in the afternoon to reduce pressure on the birds that are such a gift to the area. Today, that is the custom for a hundred miles from Wintermann's property, in abiding respect for him and as a willing sacrifice for the future along the Lower Colorado.

Chapter Four

MATAGORDA ISLAND

atagorda Island was always a mystery: remote, off-limits, inaccessible. From 1941 to 1974, the northern two-thirds of the island was managed by the Defense Department as an Air Force bombing range. The southern end of this 42-mile barrier island, which lies wholly in Calhoun County between Port O'Connor and Rockport, was the domain of Toddie Lee Wynne. The legendary Dallas oilman operated a simple but elegant cattle ranch there and entertained an impressive array of guests that included Franklin D. Roosevelt, who came for the tarpon fishing. As a result of this unique pattern of ownership, no portion of Texas' 624-mile seashore is so nearly undisturbed today as secluded Matagorda and its southerly neighbor, the island of San Jose.

Ironically, the configuration that saved this precious Texas resource from the fate of other, more developed stretches of the Gulf Coast also served to exclude virtually all public knowledge or use of the island for many years and set the stage for a fierce struggle for control of it that has spanned nearly half of the twentieth century.

29

Matagorda Island is actually a fairly new place, having been formed in but an instant of geologic time—the past five thousand years. Unlike most of the eroding Texas coast, the barrier island has continued to grow, inching ever seaward. Currents and waves arrange sand and shells, laying down a beach of unusual breadth that extends to the horizon and is unblemished by human activity. Behind the beach lie two processions of sand dunes, side by side. Here and there among them are white-tailed deer bleached nearly blond by the Gulf sun. Startled, they find cover only in the shallow swales ribbing otherwise completely flat transitional uplands between the windblown shoreline and the calm and languid bay. A single narrow road creeps down the island in this middle ground, and there is much to see in traversing it.

Small freshwater potholes along the way sustain many species of ducks in the winter and alligators all year long. The most spectacular time to be on the road is after a fire, when everything comes in to feast, including Sandhill Cranes, all manner of birds of prey—and the Whoopers.

The Whooping Cranes are the rulers of Matagorda Island, and more of them are visible here up close and personal than

anywhere else except along the Intracoastal Canal's crossing of the Aransas National Wildlife Refuge. Their habitat completes the transition from Gulf to bay in a myriad of ponds, salt flats, marshes, and channels through which flows a rich formulation that is the beginning of all marine life on the Texas coast. It was the Whoopers that ultimately brought the long-simmering battles to the surface at Matagorda, and it is because of them that its forced isolation came to an end.

In the early 1970's, efforts to develop an offshore oil and gas field in the area posed a potential conflict with military operations, and the dispute between the oilmen and the Air Force elevated the issue to national attention. Media scrutiny and the cries of concerned citizens throughout the country raised questions of what impact both of these activities might have on the majestic birds, a third of which depend on the island for wintering habitat.

As the war of words subsided, it became apparent that the primary military use of Matagorda was recreational, and the base was closed forever in 1974. Unfortunately for the public, this action sparked yet another squabble, which pitted the state against the federal government for control of the land that the original cattlemen had lost to the military during World War II.

These were no ordinary cattlemen. In marked contrast to the well-heeled lifestyle of those on the southern reaches of the island, Joe Hawes and his family had actually lived and survived on Matagorda for many generations. Storms, mosquitoes, water shortages—this land provided a hard, rough existence. Among the little evidence of human habitation that remains today are the weathered gravestones of Joe Hawes's ancestors, lying nestled behind the dunes.

On the south end of the island, Wynne, the visionary old oilman, had his eye on outer space: the only privately initiated space probe in U.S. history was launched from his pasture. On the morning of September 9, 1982, he was struck down by a heart attack at the place he loved best. As he would have wished, the countdown continued to a successful launch, and on the roadside today a rusting gantry commemorates the remarkable panache of Toddie Lee Wynne. His place was never the

same after his passing, and his heirs placed the south end into conservation forever through a transaction with The Texas Nature Conservancy in 1986.

Today things are quiet at Matagorda once again. The immense power of the beach is still there, along with the calm but teeming throb of life coursing through the marsh. A truce between the bureaucracies has resulted in public access to this most remote of Texas coastal places for the first time and to varied forms of outdoor recreation, among them hunting, fishing, birdwatching, and beachcombing. A brief trip by ferry from Port O'Connor has removed the shroud of mystery for all who are adventuresome enough to come.

And though they are both gone, the presence of Joe Hawes and Toddie Lee Wynne remains evident on the island that they loved so intensely and in such different ways.

Chapter Five

WALLISVILLE

W e scrambled up the mudbank of the Trinity River in the dense summer heat of the Texas coast. My guide was Butch Gatlin, the colonel in charge of the U.S. Army Corps of Engineers at Galveston. Affable, competent, and self-assured in his fatigues, Colonel Gatlin had landed this plum assignment in the midst of never-ending controversies here and along the Intracoastal Canal in the Laguna Madre, controversies that made the July day seem comfortable by comparison.

As we worked our way back from the riverbank through air almost as thick as the waist-high grass, the landscape was suddenly overwhelmed by the stark presence of four enormous steel structures that loomed before us like some kind of Industrial Age pyramids in a surrealist mirage. They are the gates for a set of locks that was first proposed nearly half a century ago for this stretch of the Trinity, which lies below Interstate 10 in Chambers County. Left here in monumental abandonment for more than twenty years, they are the most visible evidence of a bitter

political dispute, known as the Wallisville project, that has gripped the area for a generation.

It was named for a historic community that was situated just north of the proposed locks and dam, on the south side of the present-day freeway. The Wallisville townsite was briefly occupied by Europeans in the mid-eighteenth century, with the establishment of Mission Señora de la Cruz. Later, in 1825, a decade before the Texas Revolution, the town was established in jungle so impenetrable that the first settlers were completely unaware that the Trinity flowed placidly by just a few hundred yards away. Today the jungle has once again taken control; the last historic structures from the old settlement were moved to make way for a 20,000-acre lake, to be created by the project.

North of I-10, the project area is a vast cypress swamp, the last of its kind on the Texas coast. Meandering among the trees are watercourses and ridges that allow access to several striking but totally secluded tree-lined lakes. Colonel Gatlin and I threaded our way through the trees to Lake Charlotte, where a French trading post was established in 1754, and then we moved farther into the forest to Mud Lake, which is host each winter to nesting Bald Eagles. There is no shoreline to these hidden lagoons, only a perimeter where cypress forest meets open water. Back in the trees, the sunlight was dappled on a green patina of duckweed covering the still water, and Ibises, Herons, Egrets, and Roseate Spoonbills fluttered in and out among the stately trunks. The Spoonbills and flashing mullet in the water itself testify to the presence of salt water here in the deep woods, miles from the Gulf. As we headed back out of the trees toward the river, the tidal flow was unmistakably visible in the duckweed.

It is this fluctuating salinity throughout the 19,000-acre preserve managed by the Corps of Engineers that, for proponents, now gives the Wallisville project its underlying rationale: In the beginning, the Corps of Engineers, the City of Houston, the Trinity River Authority, and the Chambers/Liberty County Navigation District sought to flood all of the river delta marshes and woodlands to provide water for Houston and facilitate increased navigation up the Trinity. Opponents—who include conservationists, local landowners, and residents, as well as

sport and commercial fishermen—have contended for more than thirty years that the project would destroy the lovely cypress forest and forever halt the flow of life-giving nutrients, fresh water, and sediments to Galveston Bay.

Through the years of hostile litigation, changing political winds, and declining budgets, construction on the Wallisville project has been stalled, and the original engineering vision has been fundamentally curtailed. The big gate structures, like Ozymandias's broken statue on the desert, convey the scale of the fiasco.

Below the gates, we floated out into a vast deltaic marshland, which forms the north rim of Trinity Bay and provides the fuel supply for the Galveston Bay system, the most productive of all Texas estuaries. Here, alligators silently glide into the increasingly brackish water, and hundreds of thousands of resident and migratory waterfowl surge in and out year-round. All of this, and the multimillion-dollar fishery below, are dependent on the vascular system that delivers fresh water, nutrients, and sediments to them.

Today, though the Wallisville project has been reduced in scope to an even more shallow and only periodically impounded lake of some 6,000 acres, closure on the issue remains out of reach for those who have struggled on both sides for so long. Meanwhile, for better or for worse, the saltwater wedge continues to move up and down through the cypress, public use of a wonderful natural place not an hour from downtown Houston is severely limited, and the gates loom out of the weeds to remind us how grandiose and how thwarted human undertakings can sometimes be.

bicyclists, joggers, and equestrians in an imaginative alternative transportation system that connects people, communities, and nature.

While Olmsted was himself a visionary excited by the potential of the woods and waters of the Trinity, he could scarcely have foreseen its indispensable role today in protecting and reinvigorating the quality of life in the Metroplex. Throughout the Trinity's forks and meanderings, the economy will be strengthened even as the natural habitat is preserved. Through the cool green vegetation along the riverbank, I caught a glimpse of the Dallas skyline as we glided silently along, and I was reminded that Olmsted was also the person who conceived of Central Park in New York City. And I thought of the similar impact that protecting these last remnants of precious woodland will have on the future quality of life in another great American city.

Chapter Seven

BLACKLAND PRAIRIE

As settlers from Tennessee, North Carolina, and Alabama broke out of the forests of the Piney Woods and Post Oak Savannah on their unrelenting migration west across Texas, they arrived on the shores of an ocean of grass that extended all the way to the Rocky Mountains. In that time—and since the last of the glaciers— Texas was virtually all grassland. This prairie moved in the wind, blazed up and was left blackened by huge fires, and extended northward all the way up the Great Plains to Manitoba.

As one moved westward along this luxuriant continuum of meadowlands, there evolved distinct ecological differences, caused by gradually declining rainfall, increasing elevation, and changing conditions of soil and topography. At the leading edge were the tallgrass prairies of the Blacklands.

Geographically, the Texas Blacklands comprise a ribbon of rich ebony clay lying just east of the Balcones Escarpment, where the Hill Country begins, and sweeping up from San Antonio to the Red River. In the beginning there were 13 million acres of this, the most diverse of the tallgrass prairies. It took in

49

all or part of thirty-seven Texas counties—an area twice the size of Maryland. Native vegetation along this verdant band was dominated by little bluestem, a lovely grass that is only infrequently seen as blue but is just as pretty in its sorrel and flax shades of winter and is the primary indicator of natural meadow in Texas.

In a typical square mile of prairie were as many as thirty other species of grasses as well, along with fully ninety different kinds of native wildflowers of all colors and descriptions. Texas' world-famous expanses of bluebonnets, Indian blanket, coriopsis, and the rest are in fact enabled by the vegetative balance with grass. Occasionally mottes of live oak and cedar elm dappled the hillsides, but the only real forests were confined to the floodplains along the region's meandering streams and rivers.

The unique circumstances of geography and history made the Blacklands a confluence of primary cultural traditions as well. It was here in the glades that staid institutions of the Old South mingled and ultimately gave way to the wild, frightening unknowns of the western frontier. Somewhere along the line formed by today's Interstate 35, the Texas of the old Confederacy became the new land of the buffalo hunter, the cowman, and the Longhorn.

In those years, the impact of Europeans was gentle on the Blacklands; the conversion from bison to cattle left the prairies as rich and resilient as ever. Except for the introduction of barbed wire fencing and the moldboard plow—which intensified grazing and exponentially increased cultivation, giving the grass little chance to renew itself—the region might still be mostly unbroken sod.

The Blackland "gumbo" was also the most fertile ground in the world. Cotton production on the Blackland Prairie moved rapidly from that of small family farms to a massive agricultural enterprise. Driven largely by this new economic engine, the population of Texas doubled between 1860 and 1880, and a new flood of immigrants from Czechoslovakia, Germany, and other parts of Europe poured in through Galveston. Sadly, by the turn of the century, the ocean of grass was gone. Of the original 13 million acres, fewer than 5,000 now remain, the evident

result of ancient land management practices brought by Middle Europeans, who revered the beauty of their native meadows. They knew that holding back a little native hay would ensure winter feed for their livestock against drought or other natural disasters.

Today, a struggle is under way to protect the last of the Blackland Prairie. By necessity, it must focus on tiny remnant meadows, since they are all that is left. The leading force in this effort is The Nature Conservancy of Texas, which, through acquisition and conservation easement, has managed to preserve five tracts totaling nearly 500 acres.

But the surest line of defense is held by private landowners who are stewards of the native meadows—like Paul Mathews of Greenville, Mary Evelyn Blagg Huey of Wills Point, and the Woodfin family of Paris. Near Temple, Bob and Mickey Burleson—Mickey is a Parks and Wildlife commissioner—have pioneered the art of prairie restoration, successfully returning cotton fields to prairie vegetation.

Other public and private institutions in the Blacklands, including Austin College at Sherman, the City of Ennis, the Natural Area Preservation Association, and the Hearne Museum at McKinney, have also initiated prairie conservation projects. They are led by the citizens of Collin County, whose Parks Board has launched a progressive "Open Space Plan," which provides permanent protection for the beautiful Parkhill Prairie.

Thanks to these courageous efforts, a small piece of the landscape that helped define us as Texans will be there for the enjoyment and understanding of future generations. J. Frank Dobie, Texas' preeminent folklorist, knew well the importance of the great grasslands. Next to the bed where he died was a vase of little bluestem.

Chapter Eight

UPPER BRAZOS

You have to catch the water just right to make it work for you. West of Fort Worth, the Upper Brazos below Possum Kingdom Lake is affected by a kind of tide that has its origin in periodic releases from the big hydroelectric dam as the huge demand for air conditioning and thus electric power itself ebbs and flows throughout the day. Not only do these intermittent releases determine whether you will be floating contentedly along or dragging your canoe over exposed gravel, but they can also spoil the best sandbar campsite in the middle of the night—if you haven't taken the Possum Kingdom tides into account.

Despite the fundamental alteration of the very flow of the river itself, winding through the Cross Timbers between Possum Kingdom and Lake Granbury, the Brazos here remains one of the most undefiled and scenic stretches of natural waterway in Texas.

Throughout its nine-hundred-mile passage from the High Plains at Lubbock to the windblown spit on the coast where Anglo Texas began, the Brazos is the defining tie between the

55

heritage of Texas and its geography. Though we live in a time when our sense of place continues to wane, the river named by Spanish explorers for the "arms of God" defines and embraces this place, which in turn defines us in all its diversity of landscape and humanity. No other geologic feature in Texas intersects history at so many seminal points: from Stephen F. Austin's arrival to the declaration of independence at Washington, from Charles Goodnight's endless cattle range to the endless horizon first seen by Cabeza de Vaca on the rim of the Gulf.

In the best book ever written about a river in Texas, John Graves said that the Brazos "forces its ghosts upon you," an eloquent acknowledgment that along with the glories of the revolution and the cattle empire, the Brazos has flowed with the blood of slaves in the low country and Comanches on the plains. The bodies of buffalo hunters and pioneers lie along its banks as well, in a continuum of human progress at times both ugly and resplendent.

One intersection in that journey is at the Cross Timbers, which have formed the great landmark of the Western Plains. Both the Indians and the explorers, when delineating the way across the southern heartland of the continent, referred to the Cross Timbers as a kind of prime meridian, the principal guidepost between the Piney Woods and the Rockies, the dividing line between the prairies and the rolling plains. Whether early travelers approached from east or west, the Cross Timbers stretched north and south on the horizon as far as the eye could see in both directions.

Although the Cross Timbers region varies considerably in soils and vegetation, the forest is composed primarily of post oak and hickory, interspersed with mesquite. Throughout the belt are low mountains and flat-topped limestone hills covered with scrub oak, sumac, cedar, and other shinnery. At times, this topography can be steep and dramatic, and here the passage of the Brazos is most striking.

Today, in the canyons from Dark Valley to Cyclone Bend, the river hasn't changed much since the time of the Comanches. There are plenty of places to camp on the sandbars among spectacular outcroppings of rock, high bluffs, and views of the Palo

Pinto Mountains. Once threatened with total obliteration by new dams, this unique intersection of our cultural and our natural heritages renders both contemplation and adventure within commuting distance of urban Texas.

Recognizing the significance of the river and its potential for conservation and outdoor recreation here, the Brazos River Authority has begun to give serious consideration to issues of public use and access as a component of its management. An evaluation of public access to the river has been completed, Texas game wardens are on the water helping users to be safe and secure, and reservoir managers are increasingly taking recreational users into account when scheduling releases. The tide is turning on the river that ties us all together.

Chapter Nine

ROLLING PLAINS

Upstream from Possum Kingdom, on the Clear Fork of the Brazos, you get into Lambshead country. This is the Rolling Plains.

The Clear Fork, the Canadian, the Colorado, the Concho, and the Red rivers all begin here among the breaks of the Caprock Escarpment. These rivers and the creeks and streams that feed them have gradually molded and abraded the soft sands and clays of the region, fashioning its undulating character in partnership with the wind.

The people up here are seldom without the wind. They are close to the land and to their roots. Watt Mathews, who at 96 is the defining personality of the South Plains, had a sister who was born and died here before 1882. The old man is the last sibling of nine in his generation, and he still presides over the great ranch where he has lived since 1899. Historically known as the Lambshead, the ranch is managed with such respect for tradition that a different reality operates inside the gate. To this day, even strangers are welcomed to the ranch cook shack in which

Watt still holds court, a few hundred feet from the bed where he was born.

Over the hill on the Lambshead is a place called the Old Stone Ranch. Two simple and elegant but massive stone buildings sit quietly near Walnut Creek, a tributary of the Clear Fork. They were built by an audacious young U.S. Army officer, Lieutenant Newton Givens, who came to the Rolling Plains in the vanguard of government efforts to take them from the Indians in 1854. Givens apparently took advantage of his military connections and constructed the impressive Stone Ranch in 1856. It was to this place that Watt Mathews' grandparents came and settled in 1866—after Givens was thwarted in a scheme to sell beef to the Army, of which he was a highly visible soldier. From this beginning, the Mathews family began to assemble an empire that they later called Lambshead Ranch because its permanent headquarters was situated alongside Lambshead Creek, which had come to be known for a prominent mid-nineteenth-century farmer of that name.

It was cattle country, but it lay in the heart of the last great stronghold of the Indian and the buffalo. The Rolling Plains are transitional grassland that, in essence, progresses from the true tallgrass prairies in the east to the shortgrass prairies and desert grasslands to the west and southwest. This open country is basically formed of material that washed down from the Rocky Mountains during the Tertiary period. It is also called simply the South Plains.

Originally, the vegetation in this country was predominantly tall- and midgrasses, including bluestems, gramas, and switchgrass. Massive cottonwoods lined the streams in the north, where the rolling land intersects and lays open the Caprock. Farther south, in the river bottoms of Lambshead country, pecans and walnuts feed wild turkey and deer.

On this splendid veldt, the southern bison herd was extinguished in the time of the Mathews family's arrival. Sallie Reynolds Mathews—Watt's mother and the essential storyteller of the region—wrote of the hunters leaving nearby Fort Griffin in winter on long wagon trains loaded with ammunition and supplies. They returned in the spring with thousands of hides that

they stacked like cordwood in the dusty flats below the fort to await train shipment to railheads farther east. Amid the stench of the slaughter, Fort Griffin rose briefly to be a redoubt of protection on the edge of the frontier and the primary source of supplies and debauchery for buffalo hunters and soldiers. By 1875, the great cattle trail to Kansas City had shifted west to the fort, and the cowboys joined the hunters, gamblers, cavalrymen, muleskinners, con men, and loose women in the dance halls and saloons on the flats.

By 1882, General Ranald Mackenzie had finished off Quanah Parker and the Comanches, the buffalo were gone, and the railroad had come to Albany, fifteen miles away. The flag was lowered for the last time at Fort Griffin, and the intemperance of the frontier outpost evaporated, along with the smell.

Today the fort's story and that of the Mathews family is told each June in *Fandangle*, staged on the prairie west of Albany. For nearly sixty years, virtually every man, woman, and child in the community has taken part in a theatrical sharing of their heritage with each other and with all comers. The pageantry and music reflect the mystical allure of the plains and the colorful history of Fort Griffin, the lineage of the frontier families, and the firm foundation of a culture, the roots of which are still very close.

At the end of the performance, in the summer night, 96-year-old Watt Mathews joins the cast on the grassy stage and stands quietly in the wind, part of a moving tableau of art, history, and real life.

Chapter Ten

PANHANDLE

I wish I could remember the name of the man who introduced me to the secrets of the Texas High Plains. He was a packaged-meat salesman from Idalou, outside Lubbock, and five days a week he drove back and forth between all the small towns in the Panhandle, stocking the shelves of convenience stores and country groceries with bologna, frankfurters, and sliced turkey. While driving his routes during the week, he would occupy himself by making note of interesting natural features of the landscape, and on Saturdays the two of us would return to explore them.

Four hundred years earlier, Francisco Vásquez de Coronado had done the same thing—discovering, as my friend and I did, the feeling of being at sea on the Caprock itself and the humility born of contemplating the land below it. It was these sheer cliffs, marking the vast expanse of solitary flatlands above, that inspired the Spaniards to name this land the Llano Estacado, or Stockaded Plain. Later, the name was mistranslated by Anglo settlers to mean "staked plain," which led to the folklore that early travelers put down stakes behind them so they could find their way back.

69

Still, it is empty country on top, and Pedro de Castaneda, who chronicled Coronado's expedition in 1541, writes of getting completely lost because the land was so level. The High Plains were formed by the outwash of sediments coming down from the Rockies in the Tertiary period and are, geologically, the youngest formation in Texas, except for the Gulf of Mexico. The vegetation on this alluvial table is primarily short- and midgrasses, such as blue grama and buffalo grass. It was the habitat of the bison and the pronghorn antelope and today is home to the last free-ranging pure-blooded buffalo in America, saved from extinction by Charles Goodnight, the legendary Panhandle rancher and pioneer.

The loveliest natural subtleties lie in the canyons and breaks that bound the High Plains to the east, along the Caprock Escarpment, and sever it down the middle, east to west, along the Canadian River. These are the features that gave the country its name. Some of the canyon walls here reach heights of seven hundred to eight hundred feet, forming deep gorges of vividly painted rock, variegated with up to five hundred different strata. At the bottom are cool and inviting groves of huge cottonwoods that bring spectacular color to the landscape in autumn and music throughout the warm months with their clattering leaves in the ever-present wind.

The wind is always there in these canyons. It is a defining condition, along with the space and scale of the country itself. The wind, moving continuously on top and below, carries abrasives that sculpt every rock and plant in their path and add to temperature extremes that range from 20 degrees below zero to 110 above. The wind haunts places like Adobe Walls, which was the beginning of the end for the Comanches. In 1874 Quanah Parker and seven hundred warriors were turned back beside the Canadian by a handful of buffalo hunters crouched behind prairie sod and ramshackle picket structures with their 50-caliber rifles. The Battle of Adobe Walls dealt a blow to the pride and confidence of the Comanches from which they never recovered. Furious and disillusioned, Quanah Parker and his holdouts fitfully continued a hit-and-run war until 1875. They finally took refuge in the grand canyon of Palo Duro, where

General Ranald Mackenzie destroyed the Indian camp and slaughtered the captured horses. Though Quanah Parker escaped, the next year he led his starving band to the reservation in Oklahoma; it was the last chapter of the Comanchería in Texas.

After the buffalo and the Indians were gone, there began a long tradition of discounting and underestimating the steppes of West Texas, and to some extent that continues today. For example, most Texans are unaware that the state Capitol in Austin was financed not with cash but through a land trade that created the great XIT Ranch—at one time it covered 3 million acres from Lubbock to the Oklahoma border. And many do not know that this mythically flat terrain is dappled by more than 25,000 "playa" lakes—shallow and intermittent drainage basins that provide wintering habitat to more than half a million waterfowl each year, along with an equal number of Sandhill Cranes.

Today, the High Plains and Canyon Country remain among Texas' most alluring yet least understood areas. Gorgeous natural displays are preserved at Palo Duro and Caprock Canyons state parks, but there is a marked lack of accessible land in the Panhandle, particularly north of Amarillo along the Canadian River, where excellent examples of both cottonwood-lined breaks and the high buffalo country remain. Because of strong public sentiment in the region, Texans have the opportunity to leave for our children a place where they can see the bison as Coronado did. In good conscience, we should not let it pass.

Chapter Eleven

BRIGHT LEAF

On the final approach to Robert Mueller Airport, you can look out the window on the right side of the plane and see the largest tract of undeveloped land in central Austin. It is called Bright Leaf. With spectacular views of Lake Austin and the Hill Country and a constant cool breeze, Bright Leaf was for many years the retreat of an extraordinary woman named Georgia B. Lucas.

I first met Miss Lucas at her annual Christmas party on the second floor of her graceful home overlooking the lake. My friend Bob Mallouf had asked me to tag along with him because he knew I would like the hostess, who was concerned about the future of the mountain sanctuary first established by her father. Mallouf at the time was the state archaeologist and, at Ms. Lucas's request, had performed an extensive survey of the property. What Mallouf and his colleagues discovered was that the limestone ridges and breaks of Bright Leaf were typical of those inhabited by prehistoric peoples of the Balcones Escarpment, which forms the eastern boundary of the Texas Hill Country.

In the course of their reconnaissance, the archaeologists

79

concluded that the abundant water, protected camping, and plentiful food, fuel, and stone had provided the setting for at least two significant sites dating from as long ago as 1000 B.C. Mallouf also found relics of more recent occupations, extending to the early twentieth century, scattered among the ancient artifacts.

The same conditions, discovered at sites like Bright Leaf throughout the Balcones Canyonlands, have enabled the survival of some of the rarest and most endangered species of wildlife in Texas. At the time of the prehistoric occupation, the hills and steep canyons overlooking the Blacklands were themselves part of a vast tallgrass system that covered the entire Edwards Plateau. In the late nineteenth century, the naturally occurring fires were suppressed, and year-round cattle grazing replaced the intermittent impact of bison.

In less than thirty years the savannah was gone, supplanted by a dense cover of woody vegetation dominated by ash juniper, often in nearly pure stands called cedar brakes. In these woodlands nest two rare birds on the Federal Endangered Species List—the Golden-cheeked Warbler and the Black-capped Vireo. For the past several years, these species and a group of invertebrates have been at the center of an intense controversy over development in the Hill Country west of Austin. The same conditions that have attracted both humans and animals to live in the canyons and on the hilltops for thousands of years are today attracting unprecedented suburban growth to the capital city.

I believe Georgia Lucas saw it coming. Her father was a classic turn-of-the-century entrepreneur. A pharmacist by trade, he developed a cure for dengue fever and used his profits to invest in real estate in various parts of Texas. Over time, and with the discovery of oil on his property in the Panhandle, he assembled contiguous parcels of lands in the hills west of Austin, and he built his summer home at the summit of the hill now known as Mount Lucas. He died before he could finish, and his daughter, who inherited his penchant for real estate along with his assets, continued to put the place she called Bright Leaf together, piece by piece.

Today, it is one of only a few remaining large tracts in the Balcones Canyonlands that sustain the unique ecological community in the midst of the burgeoning suburbs. Bright Leaf, which provides critical habitat for the Golden-cheeked Warbler, is the core tract of a metropolitan preserve system being assembled west of town by Travis County, the City of Austin, the Trust for Public Land, and The Nature Conservancy.

It is an extremely wise investment. In the next century, this critical conservation infrastructure will guarantee some semblance of the quality of life that has distinguished Texas' beautiful capital city. The fierce determination to maintain it into the future is the most generous gift that could be made to coming generations of children in Austin.

Georgia Lucas knew that. In August of 1994 she passed away and left her family's mountainside enclave to those children, to be protected forever by the Texas Parks and Wildlife Department.

Chapter Twelve

GOVERNMENT CANYON

n a corner of the sheltered campus of Incarnate Word College in downtown San Antonio, the river that gave the city its name rises subtly from the vast and priceless underground reservoir known as the Edwards Aquifer. It flows pure and clear and with a rich diversity of invertebrate life that manifests the immaculate character of the water itself. From this beginning of understatement and innocence, the river winds its way through venerable Brackenridge Park, past crowds of tourists on the famous River Walk, on past the ancient Spanish missions to the confluence of the Guadalupe, and finally to its mouth in the estuary of San Antonio Bay. At each location, the river provides the essential element for life and culture along its banks, as it always has. Its own essential element and origin, the aquifer itself, has become a battleground among those who want and need its pure and cool abundance.

The Edwards Aquifer is a porous underground geologic formation composed of limestone; it stretches in a northward curve through south central Texas, from Brackettville to the outskirts of Austin along the Balcones Escarpment, which is the leading

85

edge of the Hill Country. The aquifer varies in width from 5 to 40 miles and is 175 miles long. Structurally, the subterranean reserve includes three fundamental components. The drainage area, or catchment, is made up of the watersheds of the Nueces, San Antonio, and Guadalupe rivers, which direct flow from rainfall downstream to the recharge area. In this highly permeable zone, water enters the aquifer itself through openings in the limestone that range from microscopic cracks and fissures to sinkholes and caves as much as one hundred feet wide.

From here the water enters the underground reservoir called the Artesian Zone, where up to 50 million acre-feet of it are stored. This subterranean treasure is the primary water source for a million and a half people, including urban, agricultural, industrial, and recreational users. The aquifer is the only developed source of water for the City of San Antonio, and it is the basis of a unique ecosystem that contains several plant and animal species considered threatened or endangered. Most of these occur at emerald and magic places where the pure water flows naturally out of the ground—at springs like Comal in New Braunfels, Aquarena in San Marcos, and the headwaters of the San Antonio at Incarnate Word.

Historically, pumping from the aquifer has been considered an inalienable right of whoever has had the good fortune to own the land above it—from farmers and ranchers to the huge city itself. But the conflicts have become increasingly bitter and divisive, pitting rural and urban users against each other and those who live over the aquifer against those who live downstream. The dispute has reached the federal courts, where plaintiffs demand regulation and others cling to free pumping as a basic private property right.

Though the courts and the Legislature have fashioned a complex management plan that may yet limit pumping for the first time, the more important question is how to protect the system itself, so that it will continue to function and there will be water to allocate.

One answer is at Government Canyon. On the way to Bandera, west of the city of San Antonio in Bexar County, lies a sector of the Edwards Aquifer Recharge Zone where, it is said, rain-

fall flows into the porous limestone so rapidly that it resembles a draining bathtub. The place has been called Government Canyon since the 1850's, when an Army survey crew camped there for four months while scouting supply routes to forts on the Texas frontier from military headquarters in San Antonio. Later, near the end of the last century, there was a stagecoach stop in the canyon, known as Old Government House or Government Station.

Today, the porous limestone, or karst country, of Government Canyon accounts for a full 5 percent of the aquifer recharge capacity in Bexar County. It is also a beautiful place. Steep slopes with dense stands of mature cedar and oak form a maze of draws and ravines, in some cases several hundred feet deep. Throughout this verdant labyrinth are fissures, sinkholes, and caves that connect directly to the vast aquifer below the surface. These gorges are also home to a wide range of Hill Country vegetation and to the endangered Golden-cheeked Warbler and Black-capped Vireo. The largest single cave chamber in Bexar County is here, refuge for a small colony of Mexican brown bats. On the floor of the canyons are great cottonwoods, elms, pecans, and walnuts, providing deep shade as well as habitat and forage for an abundance of wildlife, including Rio Grande turkeys.

Apart from the diverse beauty and natural assets of such a place within fifteen miles of downtown San Antonio, it was the recharge potential that led a unique coalition of citizens and community institutions to seek permanent protection for nearly 6,000 acres of land at Government Canyon. Recognizing that the area ranked at the very top of available properties essential to the maintenance of natural recharge and water quality, the Edwards Underground Water District and the San Antonio Water Service put up the funds necessary for its acquisition. More than forty organizations endorsed this remarkable campaign. A complex transaction, which eventually involved both the Federal Resolution Trust Corporation and the Department of Housing and Urban Development (which owned the land), was conceived and executed by the Trust for Public Land. Using matching dollars from the Land and Water Conservation Fund, Texas Parks and Wildlife completed the transaction and gained stewardship of the site, so critical to the life-giving function of the Edwards Aquifer and so vulnerable to the increased pressure of urban expansion into the Hill Country west of San Antonio.

Soon, with funding from the city, a visitors center will rise on the site and provide an introduction to the wonders hidden back in the tangled canyons beyond the gate. More important, it will be a place where the story of the Edwards Aquifer will be told and children may understand the wondrous link between the limestone draws of Government Canyon and the beautiful river that gurgles into the sunlight at Incarnate Word.

Chapter Thirteen

SOUTH TEXAS

L ike most kids who have had the good fortune to grow up in Texas, I have always responded to the magic of that place name—the King Ranch. As much as the magnitude of the real estate itself, the mythic proportions of its principal figures have been accorded a position in our culture surpassed only by those who fought for and won Texas in the revolution. This notion was abstract and remote for me until I was drawn back into the conservation business full time a number of years ago by my friend "B"—Belton Kleberg Johnson.

Captain Richard King founded the ranch in 1853. In this century, Bob Kleberg was the spread's last patriarch. Kleberg raised his nephew B, the great-grandson of Captain King, to step into those boots, grounded in a strong ethic of land and wildlife conservation. Instead, following an epic turn of events in which the family invested the leadership in another clan, B became estranged from the land and the kin who gave him his identity, and they remain unreconciled to this day. He later developed and operated his own famous ranch, the Chaparossa.

And yet at some level in this remarkable family, heritage

93

transcends even the most heartbreaking disputes—although the King Ranch and his family persist as the central elements of B's soul. Today the great ranch remains the soul of South Texas: the actual and metaphorical nucleus of a vast and diverse outdoor province that is one of the most significant natural areas in the Americas.

Minutes away from the airports at Corpus Christi and Harlingen, you can enter an outdoor realm so thoroughly distant from the urban condition that you have the sense of having traveled to a far corner of the world. The extraordinary completeness of the South Texas ecosystem results from the interplay of many factors, but chief among them are the persistent patterns of land ownership and ethics that have kept the landscape intact in large blocks, including the King, Kenedy, Armstrong, and East ranches, and the Padre Island National Seashore, which has protected the Gulf barrier island—and thus Laguna Madre itself—from the intense impacts of commercial development.

The South Texas coast has the most recent natural history in Texas, having been laid down in the Gulf by deposits of the Rio Grande, Nueces, Aransas, and San Antonio rivers. Though altered ecologically by more than one hundred years of grazing, the essential biological components and the character of the Coastal Sand Plains alongside the Laguna Madre are still there. The savannahs and prairies on the huge ranches are rhythmically accentuated by ancient sand dunes carpeted with native wildflowers and crowned by oak mottes interspersed with mesquite and acacia. Between them lie meadows of little bluestem and Gulf dune paspalum and saline flats of Gulf cordgrass; drifting across this Texas veldt, in and out of the mottes, are Texas' most fabled herds of white-tailed deer. It was here that the hunting car—a rambling open vehicle with seats on the hood and kennels in the rear—originated; today it is an integral part of quail-hunting ritual in one of the finest places for it in the world.

The coast is a world-class place for birdwatching as well. The presence of more than three hundred species has helped make Texas the number one destination for birders on the globe. The Laguna Madre, in fact, is both a thoroughfare and a haven for migratory waterfowl; winter residents include millions of birds each year, among them the endangered Peregrine Falcon, as well as 80 percent of the North American population of Redhead Ducks, which feed on the grasses of the clearest bay waters in the west Gulf.

But it is the undulating grasses of the laguna that distinguish it from all other Texas bay systems. They are the building blocks of an aquatic ecosystem that supports an annual economic contribution of $250 million to $400 million from fishing and outdoor recreation. The sport of stalking the seagrass ridges in search of schools of redfish tailing in twelve inches of clear laguna water is matched in artistry and dignity only by quail hunting across the bay among the ancient dunes.

Though private landowners have kept the terrain essentially intact, the Laguna Madre itself is at risk. The vital seagrass is dependent on clear water for photosynthesis. Unfortunately, the turbidity that threatens to block out the life-giving sunlight has been intensifying for the past several years because of increased effluent discharge into the bay and the persistence of the phytoplankton known as Brown Tide. Complicating the problem is additional murkiness caused by the disposal of dredge spoil from the Intracoastal Canal in open bay waters.

In the face of these threats, the heritage of the old ranches has reemerged in vigorous defense of the resources, as Stephen "Tio" Kleberg, King Ranch's vice president for agribusiness, has led efforts to protect the bay. In response, the government entities responsible for the dredging have joined in an effort to reduce its impact on the ecosystem in the years ahead.

The effort comes none too soon, because nowhere in Texas is the wild so within reach. The promise of the region will rest on our ability both to protect its essential character and to increase its accessibility. The continuing legacy of both culture and natural history rests largely in the hands of a new generation of private landowners no less committed than their predecessors to their own historic identity and that of the land itself.

Chapter Fourteen

DEVILS RIVER

We slipped into the river at Baker's Crossing, excited but not knowing exactly what to expect. There were four of us in two canoes. We knew that the Devils River, which heads up south of San Antonio and flows into the Rio Grande's Lake Amistad, was the most unspoiled stream in the state. We understood that the landowners along its banks would prefer that we not be there at all, and we expected the run to be a challenge. Still, we were unprepared.

The twenty-five miles of crystal-clear alternating pools and gentle cataracts between Baker's Crossing and the confluence with the Dry Devils River, where we would take out the following day, were more wild and beautiful than can easily be described.

The river is made up entirely of springflow out of the far west side of the Edwards Plateau. As we made our way downriver, both the volume and the startling clarity of the waters increased, augmented and purified by ever larger new springs merging into the stream. Each quiet pool was like paddling in an aquarium with a wide diversity of native fish available for

99

viewing, or catching, just over the side. Between the pools our
way was arduous and very tiring, for we had to drag the boats
through narrow channels too rocky to float our craft but flowing
with sufficient intensity to knock us down if we lost our footing.

This alternating ecstasy and ordeal took about twelve hours,
and there were no stops. All the land adjoining the river on this
stretch is posted, so we stood in a shallow pool to eat our lunch,
using the ice chests in our canoes for dinner tables. There are

only a few private landowners along this part of the river, and their attitude and ownership pattern, while intimidating to floaters like us, has been primarily responsible for keeping it pristine. Elsewhere along the Devils, where civilization has crept in, the toll on both the aesthetics and the environment has been extensive.

We traveled this beautiful and forbidding gauntlet all day, sometimes beside cliffs two hundred feet or more above our heads, sometimes surprising white-tailed deer just inches away from us in the lush streamside vegetation. The Devils River is a rich corridor for both vegetation and wildlife, and its diversity is enhanced by its unique transitional location at the intersection of the Edwards Plateau, the Chihuahuan Desert, and the Tamaulipan Plain.

It has nearly always been dry out here, but more so for the past seven thousand years; the vegetation that we see today has totally evolved away from that known and used by the river's original human inhabitants. Although increasingly impoverished as desertification advanced, the first aboriginal peoples of this region shared a rich and powerful culture that linked them directly to ancestral nomads from Siberia. There were cave dwellers here along the Devils and the nearby Pecos, and the remains of their uniquely spiritual rock art depicting the human-like forms of revered shamans as they ascended to the heavens still adorn the walls of many ancient shelters.

We camped for the night near another cave shelter. Although there is evidence of sporadic human activity across the ensuing centuries—including a river crossing used on the long journey of Cabeza de Vaca, the mayhem of Comanches and other tribes, and the lawlessness of a succession of desperados—the first permanent habitation since the time of the shamans occurred in this cave. It was the first home of E. K. Fawcett, who came to the Devils River on horseback from the community of Cheapside in Gonzales County when he was eighteen years old, helped put the final transcontinental spike in the Southern-Pacific Railroad near the Pecos, and founded the leading sheep-raising industry in the United States. While the impact of the sheepmen accelerated and completed the desertification of the region, Fawcett, whose name may still be seen on the wall of his cave, became the largest landowner in the region and a revered leader well into the twentieth century. He assembled an empire, the remnants of which form the unique protective barrier around the river today.

Now, though much of his domain has slipped away from his heirs, it remains in loving hands. The home ranch at Dolan Springs (which disgorges 22,000 gallons a minute into the river), today forms the heart of the 23,000-acre Devils River State Natural Area. Downstream, The Nature Conservancy has protected another 17,000 acres through purchase and conservation easements with private landowners.

We left the old patriarch's cave and put back into the river for the last leg of our trip, and I thought as we pulled away that he is resting in the knowledge that the place he worked so long and hard to assemble is protected. Each year his family still gathers at the cave for a barbecue celebrating their heritage, which began at this place.

We portaged the canoes at Dolan Falls, the largest cascade in Texas and the crown jewel of The Nature Conservancy's preserve along both sides of the river. From here, another half day's paddling and we reached civilization at the Dry Devils intersection—exhausted, proud of ourselves, and struck by the irony that a wonderful resource is available for our experience today only by virtue of the hostility of the place itself and the aloofness of the few people who live along its banks.

In the coming years, those intruders like us who would enter this extraordinary sanctuary and enjoy it must devise a partnership with the landowners that provides for limited, safe use of the river and proper respect and protection of adjoining private property. The traditional way of life on the Devils is the reason it has remained so special for us. Any strategy for using it is sure to fail if it is not firmly rooted in respect for that tradition.

I think those ancient shamans would agree.

Chapter Fifteen

SIERRA DIABLO

t was still dark when we mounted the mules and began picking our way south along the rim. We traveled roughly down the line between Culberson and Hudspeth counties in far West Texas, along the edge of a spectacular geologic formation that sweeps up the county line nearly all the way from Van Horn to the Guadalupe Mountains. As the sun began to rise on the eastern horizon, the structure, which is the predominant feature of the Diablo Mountains, became fully revealed at our feet. It is a majestic wall rising 2,500 feet from the Chihuahuan Desert floor and stretching out north and south for almost thirty miles.

My guide and companion was Topper Frank, a lion hunter and a leader of the modern private property movement in Texas. Topper and his wife and sons live in a breathtaking setting at the foot of Sheep Mountain in the Diablos, north by northwest of Van Horn, a kind of latter-day stagecoach stop on Interstate 10, two and a half hours east of El Paso. Topper, who has schooled his children at home in this remote setting, pretty much keeps to himself. He has very little use for government

and generally gets along with his neighbors as long as they stay out of his business and on their side of the fence.

Our common bond, however tenuous, was the bighorn sheep, a magnificent and highly prized big game animal that disappeared from these mountains and thus from Texas in the early 1960's. Though ultimately unable to withstand the diseases of domestic sheep introduced to the mountains by stockmen, the native bighorns made their last stand here along the rimrock of the Diablos because it is the most ideal habitat for them in the state. Eighty percent of this habitat is held by seventeen private landowners like Topper. What remains is the Sierra Diablo Wildlife Management Area, which is under the stewardship of the Texas Parks and Wildlife Department.

Like El Capitan in the Guadalupes, the Diablo Rim is a primordial coral reef formed in the Permian period and characterized by the classic physiography of basin and range. Talus slopes formed by rock debris create a transition between salt flats and vertical limestone, and talus is the bighorn's domain, providing food, precious seep water, and terrain for escape. Vegetation in this zone is primarily xerophytic shrubs, lechuguilla, and skeleton golden-eye, along with tobosagrass. Hundreds of feet above these talus slopes, Topper and I continued south in the morning sun. Here on top there is slightly more rainfall, so you encounter a few trees—piñon pine, juniper, and several small-leafed oaks. Toward noon we emerged from this scrubby mountain woodland and beheld a sight of such power and solemnity that all our differences became instantly insignificant.

Victorio Canyon was created midway along the Diablo Wall by intense fracturing and erosion over the course of a million years. The result is a work of nature so awesome and sublime that nowhere in Texas are the characteristics of the landscape more transcendent of humanity; yet nowhere are the character and identity of the mortals who have inhabited it through the years more intertwined with its power.

Victorio Canyon is the site of the last Indian battle in Texas. It bears the name of the Mescalero chief who was among the greatest Indian leaders and was the last of the Apache warriors. The local people tell many legends about exactly how and

where the final struggle of the Apache Nation occurred. One tale told at chuck-wagon campfires in these hills is that Victorio evaded the rangers and cavalry by disguising himself as a squaw, slipping up through the labyrinthine side canyons with the women and children, and then crossing the Rio Grande into Chihuahua. However he got there, the nature of his death is not in dispute. Astride a great white horse, he uncharacteristically made a target of himself and was killed by a sharpshooter in October 1880. Victorio's force and mystery still resonate in the solitude and grandeur of the canyon that bears his name.

Today, desert bighorn sheep again clamber up the walls of Victorio Canyon. The Texas Parks and Wildlife Department began efforts to reintroduce them from populations in Mexico, Arizona, and Nevada in 1970. This program has been so successful that the species, once extinct in the wild, has recovered to the point that a very limited hunting program has been permitted since 1990; sheep from the Diablos have also been moved to other suitable habitat in hopes of establishing more herds.

Thanks to the volunteer work and financial resources of the intensely dedicated Texas Bighorn Society and the determination and scientific expertise of Parks and Wildlife biologists, nearly five hundred bighorns have come back from the brink of oblivion to the talus slopes of the Trans-Pecos.

Mostly, the sheep are back in the Diablos because of a unique public-private partnership among the landowners who share their habitat. In 1990, four landowners, including Parks and Wildlife, signed an unprecedented cooperative agreement that set up the sharing of management responsibilities, costs, and benefits. They are now working out final details of another enlightened joint program, in which the income from sheep hunting will be distributed based on ownership of acres of habitat, with incentives for improvement.

Strange bedfellows, perhaps, but such commitment and investment are an extraordinary accomplishment for parties who have all too often not gotten along with each other at all. It is a relationship that will ensure not only that the sheep make it this time but also that the economic benefits of their survival provide incentive for protection of the mostly privately owned landscape that sustains them.

As Topper and I struggled on our mules back up the steep canyon trail to Diablo Rim, we looked across the chasm and saw a splendid bighorn ram standing silhouetted against the sky.

Chapter Sixteen

CHINATIS

Driving south out of Marfa in Presidio County, you pass Fort D. A. Russell, an abandoned Army post on the edge of town. Rising out of the greasewood and tobosagrass, in stark contrast to the landscape and the dusty community, are a series of massive cement structures that redefine the West Texas vista. The mammoth boxes are among the monumental works of the late Donald Judd, often described as one of the artistic geniuses of the twentieth century.

Judd's discovery of Marfa was not the first time its vast spaces and mystery had attracted those intimate with the arts. In the 1950's, the area, steeped in tradition and the ranching heritage, was briefly wrenched onto the national stage as the production location for *Giant* and the last role of American icon James Dean. Later, in the 1970's, Judd arrived with a contingent of the New York art community, principally the Dia Art Foundation. Established by Heiner and Philippa Friedrich, the foundation has a history of using breathtaking landscapes for artistic expression.

Over the next decade, the Friedrichs gradually acquired the

entire fort, including thirty-two buildings, a good part of the town itself, and some of the most spectacular mountain country in the Trans-Pecos, in accordance with the artist's expansive and singular vision. In time, whether it was because of the singularity and eccentricity of Donald Judd or for some other reason, the master and his patrons parted ways. The colossal works of art outside tiny Marfa remain today the most obvious symbols of the great gifts left to the region.

But the greater part of the legacy lies in the mountains. After the split, Judd named his artistic enterprise the Chinati Foundation—for the magnificent and secluded range south of town in which the Friedrichs had acquired thousands of acres. Rising to more than 7,500 feet above sea level, the summit of the Chinati Mountains is almost a mile above the surrounding Chihuahuan Desert floor. The peak itself is surprisingly level. It resembles a high mesa with numerous stunted oaks scattered among needlegrass and blue grama in a windblown savannah surmounted by nothing but the sky. Here you can catch an occasional glimpse of the rare Del Carmen white-tailed deer and gaze down some of the most dramatic and largely unknown canyons in the Big Bend region toward the Rio Grande and Mexico.

The most spectacular of these is Pelillos Canyon on the Friedrichs' Mesquite Ranch, and it is here in the deep gorge and in adjacent San Antonio Canyon that their intent is most evident. Situated throughout the canyon, amid intermittent waterfalls, called pouroffs, that are spectacular in autumn, are a series of simple cabins. Each is hewn of native stone and placed a sufficient distance from the next to be totally isolated, thus enhancing both the visual and the spiritual experience of the rugged topography.

This imposing terrain forms the core of the largest, most complex, and most economically important of the primeval volcanic areas of the Trans-Pecos. In one mountain pass on the eastern end of the range, the legendary Milton Faver in 1857 laid claim to all the water holes and built a chain of baronial adobe fortresses to guard against the Apaches. A hundred years later, in the same locale, more than 31 million ounces of silver

and 8 million pounds of lead were extracted from the Shafter vicinity. Elsewhere in the Chinatis there is evidence of copper, fluorite, molybdenum, uranium, and zinc. But today Shafter is an all-but-deserted ghost town beside the road from Presidio to Marfa.

And so in remote and rugged country mostly closed to outsiders, a unique collection of newcomers arrived with unconventional ideas. From fierce frontiersman Milton Faver to seminal artist Donald Judd to Houstonian John Poindexter, who has painstakingly restored as elegant hostelries three of Faver's adobe bastions, the Chinatis have always attracted people who share an individualist tradition and whose peerless marks on these mountains are certain to live far beyond them.

Chapter Seventeen

BIG BEND RANCH

The big Golden Eagle was hooded and quiet. The bird had been discovered six months before in a cornfield near the Red River town of Paris. Following the winter migration of Canada geese, the eagle had strayed far out of its range and nearly died. On this day, after weeks of rehabilitation and retraining, the eagle had arrived at Big Bend Ranch in Presidio County to be returned to the wild.

We left the ranch headquarters at eight o'clock in the morning with the eagle in a portable dog kennel. The place is called Sauceda by old-timers in Presidio County and everyone across the river in Mexico. In Spanish, the word means "where the willow grows," and the spring that nourishes the willows here is only one of hundreds on Big Bend Ranch that distinguish it from any other place in the Trans-Pecos.

We pitched and bounced in the vehicles for about an hour in the cold, dry mountain air. Driving southeast across the high country at about 4,500 feet, we passed mainly through reddish caliche terrain covered with cactus, greasewood, and sotol interspersed with stands of the native tobosagrass. Here on the

119

plateau, in the blues and grays of morning, we were in full view of the ranch's two primary geologic features, the Solitario and the Bofecillos Mountains. The Solitario is a unique and imposing topographic domed edifice with a diameter of nearly nine miles and a vast and empty depression in the center. Technically, it is called a laccolith; when the dome collapsed inward in a spectacular primordial event, it exposed limestone deposits from the Cretaceous and even older rocks formed at the southern end of the Ouachita Mountains, which stretch all the way up to Arkansas and Oklahoma.

The Bofecillos form a majestic series of ramparts ascending from the Rio Grande. They are volcanic highlands created by ash falls and flowing lava and are the source of the ranch's extensive subterranean water. Deep and dramatic canyons plunge from the heights of the Bofecillos to the river thousands of feet below.

Between the Bofecillos and the Solitario lies Fresno Canyon, the most extensive desert gorge on the ranch and the location of two of its most lovely and well-known natural assets. They are the second- and third-highest waterfalls in Texas, and as you approach them, the harsh landscape is transformed. Suddenly the canyon walls become green, and the hot silence is broken by canyon wrens and other birds darting in and out of the dense ferns and bromeliads matting the cliffs alongside Mexicano and Madrid falls, each nearly one hundred feet high and lying at the head of one of the two primary arroyos that converge in Fresno Canyon. Each is a shimmering, rainlike, fragmented cascade of life-giving water. They are among the most treasured spots in this unyielding country of breathtaking scale, pitiless conditions, and subtle revelation.

The falls are the most enchanting manifestation of the country's abundant groundwater, which is responsible for the long human habitation of this land and its unique ecological characteristics.

The first people came here between 12000 and 6000 B.C., and evidence of their presence is everywhere on the ranch, especially in shallow cave shelters, where they articulated their existence in primitive paintings on the walls. Through the

centuries, these hunter-gatherers from the mountain caves came together with prehistoric agriculturalists along the river, and the culture that evolved was undoubtedly the gentle *humanos* encountered by Cabeza de Vaca, the first European to visit Big Bend, in the sixteenth century.

From the next three hundred years, no evidence remains of any lasting or significant European settlement, except for the Chihuahua Trail, still visible today on the ranch as it winds

through the greasewood and ocotillo. This trail served for many years as the primary trade route north from Mexico to Indianola and St. Louis. Huge two-wheeled ox-drawn *carretas* were used by smugglers, entrepreneurs, and settlers to haul cargo through what ultimately became Apache country: the fierce tribe eliminated or absorbed the gentle river people, only to be pushed by settlement to its own last stand.

In this century, mining and ranching have been the dominant uses of the place we now call Big Bend Ranch State Park. Ghost towns from the mercury and silver booms still stand, along with a vast water pipeline system built by the two sheep-ranching families who assembled the ranch—the Bogel brothers and the Fowlkes. In the early 1960's, Big Bend Ranch became the fountainhead for the far-flung cattle enterprise of oilman Robert O. Anderson, who moved *coriente* cattle into Big Bend from south of the border and northward through a series of great ranches into northern New Mexico.

Today, all that remains of that empire is a token herd of 150 Texas Longhorns that continue to roam the hillsides and arroyos as reminders of a lost era. Their presence is the focal point in a struggle over symbols, of symbolism: do they belong on the natural landscape or not? This simmering dispute nettles the present transition of the land to yet another resource use.

It was hard to be disturbed by such temporal issues as we packed the eagle under our parkas to keep him warm and climbed to the very precipice of the Bofecillos to set him free. The great creature took flight, circled over our heads a few times, and headed for the massive Sierra Rica across the river. His liberation is in itself a symbol that succeeding generations will not care how we dealt with the cattle, but they will be concerned that the country was passed down to them in better condition for his renewal and for our own.

EPILOGUE

And so, as we make our way into the next century and millennium, the fate of the wonderful places through which we have defined ourselves and established our unique individuality as Texans is in our hands. All things considered, we have done pretty well as temporary stewards of the land, given what we have had to work with and the conditions we have encountered.

Increasingly, our understanding and acceptance of responsibility for the land are producing results, as private landowners, nonprofit organizations, and public agencies each develop increased capacity and, more important, strengthened commitment to stewardship. Nonetheless, much more must be done.

In Texas, no foreseeable event or circumstance will ever change the fundamental reality that the vast majority of our natural heritage will always be in private hands. Therefore, we must reinforce the ability of private landowners to protect the resources in their care. One priority should be the establishment of federal inheritance tax relief in exchange for public conservation benefits; thereby, the breakup of family lands, which is too often the inevitable result of the substantial bite taken by the government out of every estate, could be restrained.

We must enhance public access to the outdoors—not just to meet the burgeoning demand, but also to encourage access without regard to color, gender, or socioeconomic status, and to continue building a constituency for conservation among a population increasingly cut off from exposure to its natural heritage. Thoughtful and well-constructed incentives can motivate private owners to open their lands to greater outdoor recreational use. And we must make the use of our public lands more efficient both by investing in additional infrastructure and by emphasizing, wherever possible, multiple outdoor recreational use.

We must continue to build our preservation inventory by taking advantage of critical acquisition opportunities whenever they arise and by employing nontraditional techniques, such as conservation easements that guarantee permanent protection for the landscape while perpetuating private ownership. Even if we cannot gain immediate use from such procurement, we must never lose sight of our obligation to those who will succeed us.

The ability of both public and private land stewards to manage biological resources should be augmented through creation of incentives and reduction in red tape. Policymakers must support responsible means of securing the necessary funds for this purpose, because the maintenance of our natural heritage and diversity requires it.

Finally, we must acknowledge that everyone has a way to contribute and a role to play. Neither public nor private entities have a premium on responsibility. There is too much to be done and the potential of each should be expanded.

More than anything else, we must always remember that the primary beneficiaries of our work are not born yet, and we should be willing to make sacrifices on their behalf. That is the greatest privilege we have, and therein lies the opportunity to extend our abiding love of Texas beyond our own lifetimes and into the future.

Stonewall, Texas
July 23, 1995

BIBLIOGRAPHY

Abernethy, Francis E., ed. *Tales From the Big Thicket*. Austin: University of Texas Press, 1967.

Albright, Elaine Acker. "Suburban Refuge." *Texas Parks and Wildlife*, July 1993.

Baxter, David. "Big Bend Country." *Texas Parks and Wildlife*, May 1995.

————. "Panhandle Plains." *Texas Parks and Wildlife*, May 1995.

————. "Pure But Not Simple." *Texas Parks and Wildlife*, February 1993.

————. "Wild West Is No Barren Wasteland." *Texas Parks and Wildlife*, December 1991.

Bayer, Charles W., Jack R. Davis, Stephen R. Twidwell, Roy Kleinsasser, Gordon Linam, Kevin Mayes, and Evan Hornig. *Texas Aquatic Ecoregion Project: An Assessment of Least Disturbed Streams*. May 1992.

Belisle, Harold J. *An Analysis of Texas Waterways: An Analysis of the Qualities of Waterways in Texas*. Austin: Texas Parks and Wildlife, 1972.

Bentley, Mark T. *El Paso's Prehistoric Past*. 1981.

Berthelsen, Peter, Loren Smith, and Ronnie George. "Grass." *Texas Parks and Wildlife*, June 1991.

Bishop, Morris. *The Odyssey of Cabeza de Vaca*. New York: Century, 1933.

Blue Elbow Swamp. Austin: University of Texas, 1975.

Bofecillos Mountains. Austin: Lyndon B. Johnson School of Public Affairs, University of Texas, 1976.

Bolton, Herbert E. *Coronado: Knight of Pueblos and Plains*. New York: American Book, Stratford Press, 1949.

Broyles, William, Jr. "The Last Empire." *Texas Monthly*, October 1980.

Bryson, John. *The Cowboy*. New York: Garden City Books, 1951.

Burton, Harley True. *A History of the JA Ranch*. New York: Argonaut Press, 1966.

Butterwick, Mary, and Emily Lott. *Botanical Survey of the Chinati Mountains, Presidio County, Texas*. Austin: University of Texas, 1978.

Canadian Breaks. Austin: University of Texas, 1975.

Capote Falls. Austin: Lyndon B. Johnson School of Public Affairs, University of Texas, 1973.

Capps, Benjamin. *The Great Chiefs*. New York: Time-Life Books, 1975.

————. *The Indians*. New York: Time-Life Books, 1973.

Carls, Glenn E., and James Neal, eds. *Protection of Texas' Natural Diversity: An Introduction for Natural Resource Planners and Managers*. College Station: Texas A&M University, 1984.

Caro, Robert A. *The Years of Lyndon Johnson: The Path to Power*. New York: Alfred A. Knopf, 1990.

Bibliography

Cartwright, Gary. "The Last Roundup." *Texas Monthly*, February 1985.

Casey, Ethel Matthews. *Reminiscences*. El Paso: Carl Hertzog, 1979.

Champion International Corporation. *Special Places in the Forest*. Huntsville: Champion International Corporation, 1993.

Colorado Canyon. Austin: Lyndon B. Johnson School of Public Affairs, University of Texas, 1976.

Cook, Robert L., ed. *A Historical Review of Reports, Field Notes, and Correspondence on the Desert Bighorn Sheep in Texas*. Austin: Texas Parks and Wildlife, May 1991.

Correll, Donovan Stewart, and Marshall Cohring Johnston. *Manual of the Vascular Plants of Texas*. Renner: Texas Research Foundation, 1970.

Cox, Jim. "Barging Through the Laguna." *Texas Parks and Wildlife*, January 1995.

———. "Hardwoods for Dollars." *Texas Parks and Wildlife*, March 1995.

Crenshaw, Troy C. *Texas Blackland Heritage*. Waco: Texian Press, 1983.

Crouch, Donia Caspersen. "Georgia Lucas Leaves 200-Acre Treasure to West Austin." *West Austin News*, November 1994.

Dahmer, Fred. *Caddo Was . . . A Short History of Caddo Lake*. Bossier City: Everett Companies, 1988.

Dawson, Bill. "Loss of Coastal Woodlands Worries Environmentalists." *Houston Chronicle*, July 25, 1993.

———. "Water Panel Wants Wallisville Study." *Houston Chronicle*, August 10, 1988.

Dearen, Patrick. *Portraits of the Pecos Frontier*. Lubbock: Texas Tech University Press, 1993.

Denhardt, Robert Moorman. *The King Ranch Quarter Horses*. Norman: University of Oklahoma Press, 1970.

Devils River. Austin: University of Texas, 1975.

Diamond, David D. "Texas Prairies: Almost Gone, Almost Forgotten." *Texas Parks and Wildlife*, March 1990.

Diamond, David D., and Timothy E. Fulbright. "Contemporary Plant Communities of the Upland Grasslands of the Coastal Sand Plain, Texas." *Southwestern Naturalist*, December 1990.

Diamond, David D., David H. Riskind, and Steve L. Orzell. "A Framework for Plant Community Classification and Conservation in Texas." *Texas Journal of Science*, August 1987.

Diamond, David D., Gareth A. Rowell, and Dean P. Keddy-Hector. "Conservation of Ashe Juniper Woodlands of the Central Texas Hill Country." *Natural Areas Journal* 15 (1995).

Diamont, Rolf, J. Glenn Evgster, and Christopher J. Duerksen. *A Citizen's Guide to River Conservation*. Harrisburg, Va.: R. and R. Donnelley, 1984.

Dobie, J. Frank, ed. *Legends of Texas*. Hatboro, Pa.: Folklore Associates, 1964.

———. *Cow People*. Boston: Little, Brown, 1964.

———. *Tales of Old-Time Texas*. Boston: Little, Brown, 1928.

Doughty, Robin W. *Wildlife and Man in Texas*. College Station: Texas A&M Press, 1983.

Douglas, William O. *Farewell to Texas*. New York: McGraw-Hill, 1967.

Dunn, Barbara. "Life Around the Mother Lagoon." *Texas Parks and Wildlife*, June 1990.

Edwards, Janet R. "Brown Tide's Dark Shadow." *Texas Parks and Wildlife*, January 1995.

Featherston, Solon R. *True Romantic Tales of the West*. 1978.

Flanagan, Sue. *Trailing the Longhorns*. Austin: Madrona Press, 1974.

Flores, Dan. "Along the Caprock Trail." *Texas Parks and Wildlife*, August 1994.

———. "Caprock and Palo Duro Inspire Topophilia, or Love of Landscape." *Texas Parks and Wildlife*, October 1990.

———. *Caprock Canyonlands*. Austin: University of Texas Press, 1990.

Foster, Catherine Munson. *Ghosts Along the Brazos*. Waco: Texian Press, 1984.

Fresno Canyon. Austin: Lyndon B. Johnson School of Public Affairs, University of Texas, 1976.

Fries, James T. *Ecosystem Reliance on Edwards Aquifer Flow*. The Nature Conservancy of Texas, 1993.

Fritz, Edward C. *Realms of Beauty: The Wilderness Areas of East Texas*. Austin: University of Texas Press, 1987.

———. *The Great Trinity Forest*. Texas Committee on Natural Resources, Dallas, February 1995.

Fulbright, Timothy E., David D. Diamond, John Rappole, and Jim Norwine. *The Coastal Sand Plain of Southern Texas*. Rangelands, December 1990.

The Glory of Our West. San Francisco: Doubleday, 1952.

Goodwyn, Frank. *Lone-Star Land: Twentieth-Century Texas in Perspective*. New York: Alfred A. Knopf, 1955.

Gough, Buddy. "Desert Smallmouths." *Texas Parks and Wildlife*, February 1993.

Graves, John. *Goodbye to a River*. Houston: Gulf Publishing, 1991.

Green, Bob. "Salt Spring Spurs Early-Day Business." *Albany News*, June 1995.

Greer, John, Jean A. Richmond, and Mavis Loscheider. *An Archeological Reconnaissance of the Chinati Mountains: Presidio County, Southwest Texas*. Laramie: Archeological Services, 1980.

Haley, J. Evetts. *The XIT Ranch of Texas*. Norman: University of Oklahoma Press, 1967.

Hammond, George Peter. *Coronado's Seven Cities*. Denver: W. H. Kistler Stationery Company, 1940.

Harrington, Richard. "Fish Graveyard No Longer Traps Victims." *Texas Parks and Wildlife*, July 1973.

Henson, Margaret, and Kevin Ladd. *Chambers County*. Norfolk: Donning Company, 1988.

Hiller, Ilo. "The Trans-Pecos." *Texas Parks and Wildlife*, December 1975.

Holden, Frances Mayhugh. *Lamshead Before Interwoven*. College Station: Texas A&M University Press, 1982.

Howard, Rex Z. *Texas Guidebook*. Grand Prairie: Lo-Ray, 1954.

Iverson, Peter. *When Indians Became Cowboys*. Norman: University of Oklahoma Press, 1994.

Jameson, J. Franklin, ed. *Spanish Explorers in the Southern United States*. New York: Barnes and Noble, 1907.

Jennings, Dianne. "Brazos Waters Surge From State's Soul." *Dallas Morning News*, June 18, 1995.

Bibliography

Jones, Marie Beth. *Peach Point Plantation*. Waco: Texian Press, 1982.

Kenedy Memorial Foundation. Corpus Christi, 1994.
Kittelberger, Nancy. *Migratory Bird Update*. Port Mansfield: Lower Laguna Madre Foundation, 1995.
Klepper, Dan. "Trans-Pecos Tour." *Texas Game and Fish*, June 1962.

Lange, Mike. *Brazoria National Wildlife Refuge Complex Coastal Bottomlands Acquisition Proposal*. Brazoria NWR Complex, April 1993.
Langford, J. O., and Fred Gipson. *Big Bend: A Homesteader's Story*. Austin: University of Texas Press, 1952.
Lea, Tom. *The King Ranch*. 2 vols. El Paso: Guynes Printing, 1957.
Limerick, Patricia Nelson. *The Legacy of Conquest: The Unbroken Past of the American West*. New York: Norton, 1987.
Loe, Victoria. "W. Texas Site Struggling to Nourish Modern Talent." *Dallas Morning News*, February 26, 1995.
Longley, William L., ed. *Freshwater Inflows to Texas Bays and Estuaries: Ecological Relationships and Methods for Determination of Needs*. Austin: Texas Water Development Board, 1994.
Lower Colorado River Authority. *The Lower Colorado River Guide*. Austin.
Lower Colorado River Authority Land Resources Division. *A 10-Year Vision for the Colorado River Trail: 1995–2004*. January 1995.

Matagorda Island. Austin: Lyndon B. Johnson School of Public Affairs, University of Texas, 1973.
Mathews, Sallie Reynolds. *Interwoven: A Pioneer Chronicle*. Austin: University of Texas Press, 1977.
Maxwell, Ross A. *Big Bend Country: A History of Big Bend National Park*. Big Bend National Park: Big Bend Natural History Association, 1985.
McCann, Bill. *The State of the River: 1993*. Austin: Lower Colorado River Authority, 1993.
McKann, Michael H. *The Recreation Potential of Chorro Canyon: Presidio County, Texas*. Lubbock: Texas Tech University, 1975.
McNamara, Dan. *Chinati Mountains, Presidio County, Texas*. The Conservation Fund.
Meinzer, Wyman. "Shelter From the Wind." *Texas Parks and Wildlife*, June 1991.
Michaud, Stephen G., and Hugh Aynesworth. *If You Love Me, You Will Do My Will*. New York: Norton, 1990.
Mintz, Bill. "Reservoir Near Wallis Studied." *Houston Chronicle*, August 10, 1988.
Moore, Gayland A. "Wild Things." *Texas Parks and Wildlife*, October 1989.
Morrison, Richard R., III. *Environmental Issues—Water Resources: Wallisville Dam*. Galveston: Galveston Bay Foundation, February 1992.

The Nature Conservancy. *The Preservation of Natural Diversity: A Survey and Recommendations*. 1975.
Neal, James A., and Ernest S. Jemison. *The Texas/Oklahoma Bottomland Hardwood Forest Protection Program: Ecological Processes and Cumulative Impacts*. Illustrated by Bottomland Hardwood Wetland Ecosystems. Chelsea: Lewis Publishers, 1990.
Nelson, Barney, ed. *Voices and Visions of the American West*. Japan: Dai Nippon, 1986.

Newcomb, W. W., Jr. *The Indians of Texas*. Austin: University of Texas Press, 1961.
————. *The Rock Art of Texas Indians*. Austin: University of Texas Press, 1967.
Nolen, Ben M., and Bob Narramore. *Rivers and Rapids*. Garland, 1992.

Olmsted, Frederick Law. *Journey Through Texas*. Austin: Von Boeckmann–Jones Press, 1962.

Palmer, Tim. *Lifelines: The Case for River Conservation*. Washington, D.C.: Island Press, 1994.
Parisi, Phil. "Preservation Week: Celebrating Real People, Real Places, Real History." *The Medallion*. Austin: Texas Historical Commission, March/April 1995.
Parvin, Bob. "A Clear Victory." *Texas Parks and Wildlife*, June 1991.
Peyton, Green. *The Face of Texas*. New York: Bonanza Books, 1961.
Pipkin, Turk. *Born of the River: The Colorado River and the LCRA*. Austin: Softshoe Publishing, 1995.
Poole, Jackie. "Texas Mountains: High Above the Pecos." *Texas Parks and Wildlife*, October 1989.
Preserving Texas' Natural Heritage. Austin: Lyndon B. Johnson School of Public Affairs, University of Texas, 1976.

Raht, Carlysle Graham. *The Romance of Davis Mountains and Big Bend Country*. Odessa: Rahtbooks, 1963.
Ray, James D., and Loren Smith. "Waterfowl." *Texas Parks and Wildlife*, June 1991.
Reading, Robert S. *Arrows Over Texas*. San Antonio: Naylor, 1960.
Reid, Jan. "Sympathy for the Devils." *Texas Monthly*, November 1994.
Rivers, Trails, and Conservation Assistance Program of the National Park Service. *Trinity River Common Vision*. Santa Fe, 1994.
Robison, B. C. "Wallisville Dam: A Scandal in Disguise." *Houston Post*, October 19–23, 1986.
Roemer, Ferdinand. *Texas*. San Antonio: Standard Printing, 1935.
Roth, Susan. *Replanting a Forest*. The Brazosport Facts.
Rowe, James. "100 Years of Ranching: King Ranch." *Corpus Christi Caller-Times*, 1953.
Rowell, Chester M., Jr. *Natural Communities of the Rolling Plains of Texas*. San Angelo: San Angelo State University.

Sansom, Andrew. "Western Jewel of the State Parks." *Texas Parks and Wildlife*, October 1989.
Scarlett, Harold. "Wallisville Reservoir Dealt Blow." *Houston Post*, August 10, 1988.
Shannon, Manning. *Little Sandy: A Look Back*. Dallas: Performance Printing, 1992.
Sharp, John. *Texas Regional Outlook: Upper Rio Grande*. Austin: Comptroller of Public Accounts, 1992.
Sharpless, Rebecca M., and Joe C. Yelderman, Jr. *Texas Blackland Prairie: Land, History, and Culture*. Waco: Baylor University, 1993.
Simons, Helen, and Cathryn A. Hoyt. *Hispanic Texas: A Historical Guide*. Austin: University of Texas Press, 1992.
Sinclair, Robert L. "Pickerel Paradise." *Texas Parks and Wildlife*, March 1971.

Bibliography

Smeins, F. E., D. D. Diamond, and C. W. Hanselka. *Coastal Prairie: Natural Grasslands*. New York: Elsevier, 1991.

Smith, Roberta. "A World According to Judd." *New York Times*, February 26, 1995.

Solitario. Austin: Lyndon B. Johnson School of Public Affairs, University of Texas, 1976.

Steiert, Jim. "Panhandle and Rolling Plains: Wildlife Diversity Belies Flatland Image." *Texas Parks and Wildlife*, December 1991.

Sullivan, Brian D. *Migratory Bird Research and Surveys*. June 1994.

Taft, Stanley W. "Panhandle Cornucopia." *Texas Parks and Wildlife*, July 1974.

Tewes, Mike. "Coastal Refuge." *Texas Parks and Wildlife*, May 1985.

Texas Historical Commission. *You Are the Guardian of the Past*. Austin, 1993.

Texas House of Representatives. *Regulating the Edwards Aquifer: A Status Report*. Austin, July 11, 1994.

Texas Parks and Wildlife Department. *Texas Waterways: A Feasibility Report on a System of Wild, Scenic, and Recreational Waterways in Texas*. Austin, November 1973.

Thompson, Holland, ed. *The Book of Texas*. Dallas: Grolier Society, 1929.

Tompkins, Shannon. "Devils River." *Houston Chronicle*, July 24, 1994.

————. "In Houston's Shadow: Sheldon Reservoir." *Field and Stream*, May 1994.

————. "Sheldon Reservoir Makes It All the Way Back." *Houston Chronicle*, September 23, 1990.

Truett, Joe C., and Daniel W. Lay. *Land of Bears and Honey: A Natural History of East Texas*. Austin: University of Texas Press, 1984.

Trust for Public Land. *Healing America's Cities*. San Francisco, 1994.

Turner, Elsa. *Buffalo on the Frontier*. Fort Griffin Fandangle, 1995.

Turpin, Solveig A. *Pecos River Rock Art*. San Antonio: Sandy McPherson Publishing, 1991.

Twidwell, Stephen R., and Jack R. Davis. *Preliminary Assessment of Minimally Impacted Unclassified Texas Streams*. Austin: Texas Water Commission, August 1988.

Tyler, Ronnie C. *The Big Bend: A History of the Last Texas Frontier*. Washington, D.C.: U.S. Government Printing Office, 1975.

U.S. Fish and Wildlife Service. *Columbia Bottomlands Draft Land Acquisition Compliance Document*. Angleton, June 1995.

————. *Texas Bottomland Hardwood Preservation Program*. Albuquerque, May 1985.

Udall, Stewart L. *To the Inland Empire*. New York: Doubleday, 1987.

Victorio Canyon. Austin: Lyndon B. Johnson School of Public Affairs, University of Texas, 1973.

Ward, Pamela. "A Gift of Vision." *Austin American-Statesman*, November 12, 1994.

Warnock, Barton H. *Wildflowers of the Big Bend Country, Texas*. Alpine: Sul Ross State University, 1970.

Webb, Mark A., and Michael J. Ryan. "Caddo Lake: An Enduring Masterpiece." *Texas Parks and Wildlife*, March 1990.

Webb, Walter Prescott. *The Great Plains*. New York: Grosset and Dunlap, 1931.

Weisman, Dale. "Charming, Disarming Jefferson." *Texas Highways*, November 1991.

White, L. A. "Copper Breaks." *Texas Parks and Wildlife*, September 1991.

Wilbarger, J. W. *Indian Depredations in Texas*. Austin: Hutchings Printing House, 1889.

Wilke, L. A. "The Sprawling Colorado." *Texas Game and Fish*, April 1958.

Wilson, Laura. *Watt Mathews of Lambshead*. Austin: Texas State Historical Association, 1989.